Food Chain Kings

WOLVES
AND THEIR FOOD CHAINS

CHERITON
CHILDREN'S BOOKS

Published in 2023 by **Cheriton Children's Books**
1 Bank Drive West, Shrewsbury, Shropshire, SY3 9DJ, UK

© 2023 Cheriton Children's Books

First Edition

Author: Katherine Eason
Designer: Paul Myerscough
Editor: Elise Harding
Proofreader: Hayley Bennett
Illustrator: Martyn Cain

Picture credits: Cover: Shutterstock/Mjurik (foreground), Shutterstock/Artem Oleshko (background); Inside: p1: Shutterstock/M6photo; p4: Shutterstock/Stayer; p5: Shutterstock/Georg Spade; p6: Shutterstock/Melinda Nagy; p7t: Shutterstock/Keeskoopmans; p7b: Shutterstock/Volodymyr Burdiak; pp8-9: Shutterstock/Michael Wick; p10: Shutterstock/Creativex; p11: Shutterstock/AISPIX/Image Source; p12: Shutterstock/S-Belov; p13: Shutterstock/M6photo; pp14-15: Shutterstock/Agnieszka Bacal; p16: Shutterstock/Denis Pepin; p17: Shutterstock/Vishnevskiy Vasily; p18: Shutterstock/NancyS; p19: Shutterstock/KKulikov; p20: Shutterstock/Gemenacom; p21: Shutterstock/Kochanowski; pp22-23: Shutterstock/Danny Ye; p24: Shutterstock/S Eyerkaufer; p25: Shutterstock/Scott E Read; p26: Shutterstock/Stayer; p27: Shutterstock/Moosehenderson; p28: Shutterstock/Pi-Lens; p29: Shutterstock/Thomas Barrat; pp30-31: Shutterstock/Giedriius; p32: Shutterstock/Daniel Eskridge; p33: Shutterstock/Volodymyr Burdiak; pp34-35: Wikimedia Commons/Jonathan Chen; p36: AdobeStock/Hakoar; p37t: Dreamstime/Twildlife; p37b: AdobeStock/Chris; p38: Dreamstime/Albertoloyo; p39: Dreamstime/Tatiana Belova; p40: Dreamstime/Marcel Schauer; p41: Dreamstime/John Wollwerth; pp42-43: Shutterstock/Alex Satsukawa.

Printed in China

Please visit our website,
www.cheritonchildrensbooks.com
to see more of our high-quality books.

CONTENTS

CHAPTER 1

KILLER KINGS

Wolves once lived almost everywhere on land, but today they are most common in very wild places. These incredible hunters live in different areas of the world. They are found in the northernmost part of Earth, the icy Arctic, but they also live in the hot **deserts** of the Middle East.

Chain Champs

Wolves are part of food chains in the habitats in which they live. A food chain is a series of animals and plants that are connected because they depend on each other for food. Each animal in a food chain is linked to the animals and plants below it. Wolves are at the top of many food chains because they **prey** on elk, moose, and other animals that live in the forests. The animals they prey on feed on plants, such as shrubs, grass, moss, and pinecones. The wolves, moose, and plants form a food chain. Wolves are at the top of the chain and the plants, which make their own food from sunlight, are at the bottom of the food chain.

Wolves usually hunt in pairs, or in a larger group of wolves, called a pack.

This huge area of pine and fir forests is found south of the Arctic Circle. Packs of wolves live and hunt in these forests.

Forest Kings

Wolves are killer kings of the huge **coniferous** forests that stretch across northern Canada, Alaska, Asia, and northern Europe. Their howls echo through the pine and fir forests in these places. Wolves live farther south, too, in **deciduous** forests and the **grasslands** around them.

Links in the Chain

Food chains are made up of producers, consumers, and decomposers. Animals that eat other animals are called secondary consumers, and the plant-eating animals they eat are called primary consumers. The plants that primary consumers eat are called producers. Decomposers break down the waste produced by consumers and producers.

Hunting Family

Wolves belong to the dog family, which also includes wild dogs, coyotes, jackals, and foxes. All pet dogs are thought to have come from wolves. German shepherd dogs and huskies still look like wolves, but most pet dogs now look very different from wolves.

NO WASTE WOLVES

Wolves usually eat all of their prey, even the bones! If they do leave any remains behind, they help feed other food chains. Wolf kill remains are eaten by grizzly bears, bald eagles, and many other scavengers that feed on dead animals.

Huskies live happily in the snow and are often used to pull sleds.

Lemmings are always on the lookout for their enemy, the wolf.

The gray wolf has patches of white fur, which help camouflage it against the patchy snow where it lives.

Camouflaged Killers

Gray wolves, or timber wolves, have gray, brown, and black fur. Arctic wolves live north of the forests in North America and Greenland. They are colored white, which camouflages, or hides them, against the snow that covers the ground in these places for most of the year. Arctic wolves prey mostly on caribou, musk oxen, and Arctic hares. They also snack on smaller animals, such as lemmings, and may even catch seals and birds, such as ptarmigan. They eat all of their prey, even the bones!

Southern and Smaller

The size of wolves depends on where they live. For example, larger wolves are found in Canada, Alaska, and across northern Asia. Smaller wolves survive farther south, such as in the Rocky Mountains of North America or the mountains of Ethiopia, in Africa.

7

WHITE WOLF HUNTER

Like all wolves, Arctic wolves are social animals. That means they like to be with other wolves. Arctic wolves live in packs of between seven and eight animals. They are powerful hunters that can take down prey as large as caribou.

Arctic wolves can travel much farther than other wolves to hunt for food, and are perfectly **adapted** to seek out prey in their snowy, freezing homes. The Arctic wolf can keep its paws at a temperature that is lower than the rest of its body. That stops the paws from losing too much heat, even as the wolf races across the frozen ground. At the same time, blood pumps from the hunter's body into its paws, to stop them from becoming too cold.

During the winter, Arctic wolves grow a second layer of fur to protect themselves from the cold. Their white fur camouflages them perfectly against the snowy ground they run across.

Wild No Longer

The Arctic wolf is one of the few wolves that rarely meets a human. That is because its habitat, or the place in which it is naturally found, has few people because it is such a difficult **environment** in which to live. However, that is changing as more people travel to the Arctic to search for resources, such as gas and oil.

Roads, mines, and pipelines are being built in the Arctic, bringing people to the area and damaging the wolf's environment. Any change to a **predator**'s **territory** can cause disruption in its food chain, and industrial development in the Arctic is damaging the wolf's food supply.

Another threat to Arctic wolves and their food chains is **climate change**. Weather changes in the Arctic are making it more difficult for Arctic hares and musk oxen to find food. Both animals are prey for the Arctic wolf, and as their numbers decline, so too might those of the wolf.

Where in the World?

Arctic

North America

IN THE FOOD CHAIN

Arctic wolves eat a wide variety of food. Meals are scarce in the Arctic, so the wolves must hunt and eat what is available. The wolves eat musk oxen and caribou, but will also eat Arctic hares, lemmings, ptarmigan, and small animals such as nesting birds.

Arctic wolf food chain

ARCTIC WOLF

CARIBOU

LICHEN

DESIGNED TO KILL

Wolves are designed to be a top predator. They have sharp senses, and their bodies are streamlined and well-camouflaged. They have powerful muscles, strong backs, and can run very quickly. They can also keep running for a long time, which allows them to chase prey until it is tired. Then, the wolves pounce on the victim!

Streamlined Killer

A wolf keeps its head low and level with its shoulders as it runs. This streamlined shape allows the animal to move fast, and its large paws can grip onto different types of ground as the wolf runs. Wolves have bristly hairs between their toes, which helps them move across the snow. Their blunt claws can also grip onto slippery rocks.

A wolf uses its strong senses of smell, hearing, and eyesight as it carefully stalks its prey.

Speedy Hunter

Wolves can run for hours at 5–10 miles per hour (8–16 km/h), which helps them cover large areas while looking for prey. They can also burst into a terrifying sprint of up to 37 miles per hour (60 km/h) to bring down animals.

ULTRA-RUNNER

The wolf is designed to travel over long distances for a long time. It has long legs, big feet, and a deep-but-narrow chest. Wolves can chase after their prey for many hours, over many miles. In just one day, wolves can travel up to 50 miles (80 m). They are truly long-distance hunters.

With its head bent low, a wolf can run quickly across the snow.

Super Senses

Of all their incredible senses, wolves use their amazing senses of smell and hearing the most. Their sense of smell is 100 times better than a human's, and they can pick up smells that are more than 1 mile (1.6 km) away! Wolves can even hear better than dogs and can pick up sounds that are up to 10 miles (16 km) away.

Night Stalker

Wolves are nocturnal animals, which means they are active at night and sleep in the day. Wolves cannot see things that are far away, but can see well over short distances. They usually hunt in the dark, and see better at night than during the day. A wolf's sight at night is several hundred times better than that of a human's. The wolf's night vision is one of the best of all animals on Earth, which is another reason why they are a top predator.

Light reflects off the back of a wolf's eyes to help it see better in the dark.

EYES ON!

FREE FOOD FINDER

Wolves use their intelligence to help them find food. Early settlers in North America noticed that wolves often followed them as they hunted. The wolves hung back until a bison was killed, then moved in to snatch a free meal. Native American people admired the wolf for its smart skills, but European settlers were scared of the creature and hunted it over time.

Super-Smart Hunter

Wolves have one more big advantage over their prey—they are smarter than most of the animals they hunt. Wolves are one of the most intelligent predators on Earth, and many scientists believe they may even be 10 times smarter than the smartest dog.

As wolves run, they listen out for the sounds of other wolves as well as those of prey.

STREAMLINED HUNTER

The gray wolf is the biggest wolf in the world. An adult male can grow to about 6.6 feet (2 m) long, from the tip of its nose to the tip of its long, bushy tail. It weighs up to 143 pounds (65 kg). This large animal is a super-swift and powerful predator.

Gray wolves are perfectly adapted to the different habitats in which they live. They are found in many different parts of the world, from North America through Asia and the Middle East. The wolves have streamlined bodies, with narrow chests and elbows set closely together. Their slim-but-powerful shape helps them run speedily after prey through snow, brush, or rocky places.

Gray wolves live and hunt in packs of between two and 15 animals. These smart killers adapt their hunting plans to suit whatever prey is nearby. The wolves can bring down animals as large as deer, elk, bison, and moose. But if big prey is scarce, they will feed on any dead animals they find.

Helpful Hunter

When gray wolves were released into Yellowstone National Park, scientists were surprised to find that the number of pronghorn antelope increased. Wolves prey on pronghorn, but coyotes prey on pronghorn fawns. The pronghorn herds in the Park benefitted because the wolves chased away the coyotes, so more fawns were able to survive to adulthood.

Not only do the gray wolves help protect pronghorn groups within the Park, they also provide food for many other animals there. Cunning coyotes wait until the wolves have finished feeding on their prey, then when the wolves have left, the coyotes eat what remains. Other animals too eat what the wolf does not, including ravens and magpies. Bears also feed on any leftovers.

Where in the World?

North America

Yellowstone National Park

IN THE FOOD CHAIN

Gray wolves feed on a wide variety of food, including large prey such as deer, elk, moose, bison, bighorn sheep, caribou, and musk oxen. They also eat smaller animals such as beavers, hares, and fish.

Yellowstone gray wolf food chain

GRAY WOLF

PRONGHORN

SAGEBRUSH

KILLER BODIES

A wolf's fur keeps it warm and blends in with the wolf's habitat. Northern wolves, which live in the coldest places, have two layers of fur. A thick, fluffy undercoat keeps the wolf warm in winter. On top of the undercoat is an outer layer of long hairs. Snow and water slide off the long hairs to protect the undercoat beneath.

Light and Dark

Gray wolves have gray-brown fur with light and dark patches. The colors camouflage the wolves against rocks and trees. Wolves that live deep in the forest are almost black to match their dark surroundings. Arctic wolves are white so they can hide against the snow.

An Arctic wolf's thick white fur keeps it warm and camouflages it against the snow and ice.

Big and Bushy

In northern areas, male wolves can grow to a length of around 6.6 feet (2 m) long, from the tip of their nose to the tip of their long, bushy tail. From their feet to the top of their shoulders, the animals can reach a height of around 30 inches (76 cm), and weigh up to 143 pounds (65 kg). Female wolves do not grow as large, and on average are 20 percent smaller than the males.

This wolf looks as if it is fast asleep, but its ears are pricked to catch any sounds.

Always Alert

Wolves are so well **insulated** by their fur, they survive through winter without a **den**. They just curl up on the snow, put their noses between their back legs, and cover their faces with their bushy tails. Their ears remain pricked, however, alert for sounds of danger or prey.

Wolves hide among trees as they stalk prey through the forest.

Picking off Prey

Wolves hunt mostly at night, from dusk onward. They use their sense of smell to find their prey. When the wolves pick up the scent of the prey, they **track** it. They try and creep up to a herd of animals without being spotted.

KILLING TO EAT

In Minnesota, gray wolves prey mostly on whitetail deer, but they also catch moose, beavers, and snowshoe hares. Wolves kill only as many animals as they need to survive. In Minnesota, it is estimated that about 3,000 wolves kill about 50,000 deer a year. That's about the same number of deer that human hunters kill.

Hardworking Wolves

Wolves work as a group to track their prey, helping each other to make sure that a hunt has a good chance of success. The pack may track a herd of prey for days before they make their move on it. All the time, they look at the herd, figuring out what animal may be young or old, and what might be sick or injured. Wolves always target the weakest animals in the herd, because they are the easiest to bring down.

Staying Alive

Once they have pinpointed their target prey, the wolves try to separate the animal from the rest of the herd. Sometimes, a herd of large animals, such as musk oxen, stand their ground and protect the weaker animals. If this happens, the wolves often give up the hunt. The smart animals know that it is better to wait for another day than risk being injured or killed by an angry herd.

Reindeer fawns often keep watch in opposite directions to look out for wolves that might try and attack them.

ALL CLEAR THIS SIDE!

Watch the Wolf

When wolves hunt, they wag their tails excitedly. They move toward the animal they are tracking with the wind in their faces, so the prey is less likely to smell them. If the animal spots the wolves and runs, the wolves chase after it. Lighter and smaller female wolves often herd the animal, darting back and forth in front of it to confuse it and keep it from escaping. Larger, more powerful wolves then lunge at the prey.

WOLFING IT DOWN

Each wolf needs about 3-10 pounds (1.3-4.5 kg) of meat a day, but can eat up to 22 pounds (10 kg) in one sitting. A big meal will last a wolf for several days. Wolves eat quickly. They want to finish their meal before larger animals, such as grizzly bears, try to steal their kill.

Wolves show their huge, sharp fangs as they get ready to attack.

Grab and Kill

If they catch the animal, the wolves grab it and kill it with their sharp teeth and strong jaws. They rip through the flesh, eating the best parts first. These include the rump and the soft insides of the body, such as the heart, the lungs, and the liver.

Deadly Hunting

Hunting is a dangerous activity for wolves. Their bones can be broken if an animal such as an ox or a deer kicks out, and antlers can deliver painful and deadly slashes. If a wolf's jaw is broken during the hunt, it will be unable to feed, and could die.

Wolves hunt both large and small prey, including rabbits.

A HUNTED HUNTER

The Indian wolf has **descended** from wolves that first began to live in India and other parts of Asia more than 800,000 years ago. It is one of the world's smallest wolves, growing to a maximum of only 38 inches (96 cm) tall and weighing between 40–60 pounds (18–27 kg).

These small-but-smart wolves often work in pairs to hunt. One wolf distracts the prey, while the other wolf attacks the unsuspecting animal from behind. Indian wolves are nocturnal animals. The night-time hunters stalk prey in the grasslands, forests, and scrublands where they live.

The Indian wolf has long legs and a slim face. Its fur is shorter and thinner than the fur of wolves that live in northern parts of the world. The wolves are colored brown and fawn, with patches of gray.

Asia

Breaking the Chain

Only 2,000 to 3,000 Indian wolves live in the wild today. There are so few of them that they are protected as an **endangered** species. The wolves' numbers have shrunk because the animals the predators fed upon in the past have mostly died out—they were hunted to **extinction** by people. That has left the wolves with little to eat, and as a result, the animals have turned to farmers' livestock, or farm animals, for food.

The Indian wolf is an example of how damaging a food chain can lead to a series of disasters, both for animals and people. As the wolves have fed on farmers' animals, people's dislike of the wolves has grown. Farmers have poisoned the wolves to stop them attacking their livestock. The hungry and desperate wolves have even been known to attack children, and local people have hunted the animals as a result.

IN THE FOOD CHAIN

Before the Indian wolf's natural food chain was so badly damaged, it fed on prey such as antelopes, rodents, and hares.

Indian wolf food chain

ANTELOPE

GRASS

INDIAN WOLF

CHAPTER 4
PACK KINGS

Most wolves live together in packs of 8 to 15 wolves, but packs of between 6 to 10 animals are most common. Each pack includes a male, a female, and their offspring. The male and female are in charge of the group, and are called the alpha wolves.

Who's the Boss?

The alphas make sure all the wolves in the pack know the alphas are in charge. They also organize the group. Every wolf in the group has a role to play, and a particular position within the pack. Sometimes, a male wolf will live on its own, as a lone wolf, until it finds a female to **mate** with. Then, the male and female wolf begin a new pack.

The male wolf here is the biggest wolf in the pack.

I'M TOP DOG!

Pup Protection

Before a female wolf gives birth, she finds a den. She may use an old den, or may make a new one in a riverbank or between the rocks. When her pups are born, the whole pack cares for them for the first eight months, until the pups are old enough to hunt with the pack. The alpha female organizes the care and protection of the pups, while the alpha male finds food for them.

Hungry grizzly bears are a great threat to wolf cubs.

PUPS IN DANGER

Wolf pups are not top predators. They are often preyed on by golden eagles, grizzly bears, and black bears. Bears may dig through the earth to reach the pups in their dens. Adult wolves try to protect the pups by distracting the bears.

Wolf Talk

The sound of wolves howling can be heard for long distances. Wolves howl to call together members of their pack and to tell each other danger is nearby. Like dogs, wolves also bark, growl, and whine to talk to each other. They also use body language to send messages.

Top Dog

A wolf pack is social and very organized. Each member has a special rank. The strongest male and female wolf are at the top of the group and are the alphas. Weak wolves are at the bottom of the pack. The pecking order of the pack has a purpose—it stops the wolves from fighting among each other and injuring one another. With the alphas in charge, the pack can work with cooperation, and therefore each wolf within it has a better chance of survival.

When one wolf howls, other wolves join in! Wolves howl the most in winter.

HOWLING HUNTERS

The sound of wolves howling is one of the most terrifying of animal sounds. Wolves howl mainly to warn other wolves to keep away. However, for hundreds of years humans felt so threatened by wolves and their howling that they killed them whenever they could.

Young wolves like to play and wrestle together. They do so to learn which wolf is stronger and which is weaker.

Weak and Strong

Wolves use body language to show their rank. A strong wolf holds its tail high, while a weaker wolf **submits** by crouching low or rolling onto its back. When a wolf rolls onto its back, it exposes its chest and belly to the **dominant** wolf. This puts the weaker wolf in a vulnerable position, and shows that it is submissive. Weaker wolves may also lick the muzzle of the alphas and tuck their tails between their legs.

Special Smells

Smells are very important to wolves, especially their own smells. A wolf pack has its own territory, which it defends against other wolves. Wolves mark the edge of their territory with strong smells to warn other wolves to keep away.

Making a Mark

Wolf smells are made by special glands at the top of the wolf's tail and in its paws. When a wolf urinates, it often scratches the ground afterward. The scratching probably gives off very strong-smelling chemicals from the glands in the wolf's feet. Wolves mark their territory by urinating and by scratching tree trunks. Each wolf smells different, so members of the pack recognize each other by their smells.

ROAMING RANGE

The size of a wolf pack's territory varies a lot depending on where in the world it is. For example, a wolf pack in Minnesota might prowl a territory that ranges between 25-150 square miles (40-240 sq km), but a wolf pack in Canada can travel across a territory between 300-1,000 square miles (480-1,600 sq km).

These footprints were left by a wolf. Even if wolves cannot see another wolf's track, they can still smell it.

A wolf finds out about other wolves and possible prey by smelling the ground.

Saved for Later

Wolves often save food and bury it somewhere safe, in case they cannot hunt or find food for a while. These hidden stores of food are called caches. Wolves often save around 15 pounds (6 kg) of any meal, so they or other wolves in the pack can eat it later. If the cache is eaten and none remains, wolves mark the area to show other wolves in their pack that the food store is empty. That stops them from wasting time digging there.

AFRICAN HUNTER

The Ethiopian wolf is the only wolf that lives in Africa. It is slim with long legs and reddish fur. It grows to a length of up to 3 feet (1 m) and weighs up to 40 pounds (18 kg).

Unlike other wolves, the Ethiopian wolf hunts alone. It spends part of its day with fellow wolves, but spends the rest searching for food on its own. The wolf mainly hunts and eats rodents that live in its habitat. The wolf's food includes hares, grass rats, and giant mole rats. It also hunts and eats goslings, and will eat eggs and the remains of any dead animals it finds. Although it mainly hunts alone, the Ethiopian wolf sometimes joins forces with other wolves to hunt larger prey such as antelopes and lambs.

The Ethiopian wolf is a lot lighter and thinner than wolves that live farther north.

Africa

Ethiopia

Last of the Wolves

The Ethiopian wolf is found only in a few mountainous parts of Ethiopia. With fewer than 550 wild animals left, the wolf is at threat of extinction and is listed as a **critically endangered** animal. There are so few wolves left because they have been hunted by people. The animals have also lost a lot of their natural habitat, because people have taken it for farmland. Disease has killed many of the wolves, too. The Ethiopian wolf is often infected with rabies, which it catches from local dogs.

IN THE FOOD CHAIN

The Ethiopian wolf has adapted to suit the food supply in the mountains of Ethiopia. The wolf has developed a slimmer muzzle and more widely spaced teeth than wolves that live in northern parts of the world. That is because small prey such as hares and rats hide in burrows in the Ethiopian mountains. The wolf uses its narrow muzzle to reach into burrows, and its widely spaced teeth grip onto the prey inside.

Ethiopian wolf food chain

EARTHWORM

ETHIOPIAN WOLF

GRASS RAT

CHAPTER 5

PAST PREDATORS

Wolves have a long and complicated past, and scientists have different views about where wolves came from. Some believe that early wolves came from North America, then spread to Asia and South America. Others think the wolves traveled from Northern Europe to North America.

Wolf Story

Most scientists believe that wherever they first came from, wolves **evolved** from much earlier and smaller animals, which were about the size of a gopher. Over time, they changed into larger creatures, with the first wolves prowling on Earth about 60 million years ago. From then onward, wolves continued to develop and change. Around 2–3 million years ago, the wolves that were the distant relatives of modern-day wolves were born.

Just like the wolves of today, ancient wolves were fierce hunters. They also lived in packs and hunted as a group.

Ancient Journey

The first gray wolf probably appeared about 1 million years ago. It lived in an area that is today Europe and Asia. Around 750,000 years ago, it may have journeyed to North America, and became the **ancestor** of the modern gray wolves that live on the **continent** today.

The gray wolf was able to adapt to its changing world, and therefore survive.

GRAY KING

Before the gray wolf evolved, another wolf-like predator stalked North America. It was called the dire wolf, and it probably lived alongside the gray wolf for about 400,000 years. The dire wolf was an awesome **prehistoric** hunter, but unlike the gray wolf, it could not adapt to its changing environment. When the dire wolf died out, the gray wolf became the killer king of North America.

ANCIENT HUNTER

At the time it lived, the dire wolf was one of the most powerful predators on land. It was twice the size of a modern gray wolf, and had an incredibly powerful bite. This prehistoric predator could even crush bones in its jaws!

The dire wolf probably hunted in packs, like modern wolves. It likely seized its prey in its huge jaws, then killed it by biting it over and over again. The animal had an incredibly powerful bite force—scientists have calculated that it was almost 130 percent more powerful than that of the biggest modern-day wolf, the gray wolf.

The dire wolf was a formidable hunter, but it was also smart at sniffing out leftovers. Evidence shows that the animal probably fed on the remains of kills left behind by another prehistoric super-predator—the sabre-toothed tiger!

This is the skeleton of a dire wolf. The animal had a large body with powerful jaws.

Ice Age End

Dire wolf **fossils** have been found in North and South America. Scientists studying the animal believe that the last of its kind died out around the end of the last **Ice Age**. As Earth became warmer, and the ice began to melt, the creature's environment changed quickly—and so did its food chain. Many of the animals that the wolf preyed on, such as mammoths, began to die out. They were also possibly hunted by early Americans, leaving little food for the dire wolf. As its food chain crumbled away, the dire wolf could not adapt, and it too disappeared.

Where in the World?

North America

South America

IN THE FOOD CHAIN

Dire wolves were big animals, and they ate big prey. They fed mainly on horses, but also hunted and ate camels, bison, and mammoths.

Dire wolf food chain

DIRE WOLF

HORSE

BROADLEAF PLANT

CHAPTER 6

FOOD CHAIN FIGHT

Wolves do not hold complete power at the top of their food chains. Wolves are scavengers as well as hunters. This means that they feed on dead animals when they can, and compete with other scavengers for food. Other scavengers include grizzly bears, coyotes, and cougars.

Bears and Wolves

Bears and wolves come into contact often because they share the same territory. They may fight each other for control of that territory, and the food within it. The animals prey on each other's babies, and bears often try to drive wolves away from a recent kill so that they can eat it themselves. Bears will be especially aggressive toward wolves when protecting their bear cubs.

Brown bears will chase away any nearby wolves to defend their cubs or their food.

Cougars may look cute, but these animals are fierce fighters and will attack wolves to defend their young.

LUNCH LEFTOVERS

Many animals eat food left by wolves. Coyotes, foxes, and weasels quickly move in to feed on the remains of a wolf's meal. Ravens hang around while the wolves eat, waiting for leftovers.

Big Cat Danger

Wolves also face another killer king in their territories—big cats. In parts of Asia, wolves may come into contact with the Siberian tiger. This ultra-killer will hunt and kill wolves, and steal their food. It is no surprise that wolf populations are low in places where the tiger lives.

Cougar Kills

In North America, another big cat poses a danger—the cougar. However, despite the danger, wolves sometimes try to steal a kill from a cougar. If the cougar fights back, it can injure or even kill a wolf. Wolf packs will try to drive cougars away and may kill any that come into their territory.

Coyotes often wait for wolves to finish eating, so they can steal the remains of the wolves' meal.

Breaking the Chain

Wolves have few natural predators, because the food chain kings are feared by most animals they come into contact with. These impressive hunters can live in the wild for up to 13 years, because they are not prey for most other hunters. However, humans have changed all that.

Hunted by Humans

Humans have always been the biggest threat to wolves. At one time, wolves were the most widespread **mammals** after humans. But when most humans came into contact with wolves, they started to harm wolf populations. Then, when humans began to farm animals near wolf territory, the smart wolves realized farm animals were easy prey. They began to hunt them. As a result, farmers protected their animals by killing the wolves.

With fewer than 500 Ethiopian wolves still living in the wild, these are the most endangered of all wolves.

Starving to Death

Into modern times, people have killed wolves, damaged their habitats, and killed their prey. Many wolves are now in danger of extinction. Wolves have lost their prey because people shot the large animals, such as bison and moose, wolves preyed on. People also brought in cattle, sheep, and other farm animals to graze the land. That changed the natural **ecosystems** in wolf territory, and damaged food chains by driving out the wolf's prey. Today, one of the biggest causes for the drop in wolf populations is starvation.

TRAPPED AND KILLED

Arabian wolves live in a few scattered groups in the Middle East. They hunt hares, gazelles, and ibex, and scavenge whatever they can. They also attack small farm animals, such as lambs and goats. For this reason, farmers trap and kill the wolves whenever they can.

Wild red wolves became extinct in the wild in 1980. The wolves have since been bred in captivity and were released into North Carolina in 1987.

Gray wolves are now free to prowl in Yellowstone National Park.

PART OF THE CHAIN

Wolves are also food for other animals. When wolves die, other predators and scavengers may feed on the animals' remains. For example, grizzly bears and bald eagles have all been known to eat the remains of dead wolves, which helps the creatures survive. That in turn keeps their food chains strong.

Survive and Thrive

You might think that it would help animals such as deer and caribou if there were no wolves to prey on them. Scientists have found that this is not so. Food chains are complicated, and if just one animal in a food chain disappears, it has a big effect on all the other animals in the chain.

Healthier Herds

Wolves are important to their food chains and environments for many reasons. Wolves hunt and eat sick, old, and weak animals in a herd. That makes sure that the remaining animals in the herd **breed** only with healthy animals, and as a result, healthier babies are born. That helps the entire herd survive into the future.

Food for All

Wolves also control the numbers of plant-eating animals. Without wolves to hunt them, those animals might grow too great in number. They would then eat too many plants, which would damage a food supply for all the other animals that rely on those plants. Wolves help maintain a balance of food in the areas in which they live, and that protects the food chains there.

Saving Wolves

Thankfully, today people are becoming more and more aware of the importance of wolves in their ecosystem. Now, wolves in some areas, such as Yellowstone National Park, have been given protection so they can continue to rule their food chains.

Kings Forever

Earth's ecosystems are fragile, and the wolves within them have faced a real threat for a long time. Today, we understand more than ever that wolves are important animals, because they have a crucial role to play in their ecosystems. To keep our planet healthy, we need to protect every link in Earth's food chains, including the killer kings at the top of them.

Wolves may hunt pronghorn antelope, but the antelope do better alongside wolves because the wolves keep their food chain in balance.

HAIRY HUNTER

The maned wolf was considered to be a wolf for a long time, but recent **genetic** studies show that it is not a true wolf, but rather a large **canid**, like a wolf. The animal looks very like a wolf, with its thick mane of dark hair, which is how it got its name.

The maned wolf does not live or hunt in packs. Instead, it lives in pairs of a male and a female, which share a territory. The pair hunt by stalking small animals through the grassland, then pouncing on their prey. The maned wolves seize the animals in their jaws, then kill them by biting them on their necks and shaking them violently. The animals eat their prey by jabbing and tearing at its flesh with their long, sharp teeth.

Maned wolves have very long legs, a red-and-black coat, and a narrow muzzle. Their jaws are full of sharp teeth as well as flat molars, which they use to crush fruit.

South America

Territory Threats

The maned wolf lives in grassland in Brazil, Paraguay, Argentina, Bolivia, Peru, and Uruguay. The animal has adapted to live and hunt in its habitat—its ultra-long legs help the animal see over the tall, thick grasses, so it can spot its prey.

Today, there are only about 2,000-4,500 maned wolves living in the wild. The animals are under threat because they have lost so much of their land due to farming and ranching. Roads have been built through the wolves' territory, and the animals are often hit and killed by cars. Like wolves around the world, these apex predators and their food chain are threatened because of the changes that people have brought to them.

IN THE FOOD CHAIN

Maned wolves feed mainly on small prey. They hunt birds that live in the grassland and hook fish from rivers with their long muzzles and sharp teeth. They also feed on plants such as sugarcane, tubers, and fruit. The wolves even eat insects!

Maned wolf food chain

RIVER PLANT

MANED WOLF

FISH

ULTIMATE KILLER!

WHO IS THE ULTIMATE KILLER KING OF THE WOLF KINGDOM TODAY? CHECK OUT THE FOOD CHAIN FACTS BELOW, THEN YOU DECIDE!

ARCTIC WOLF

AVERAGE LENGTH	3–6 feet (91 cm–1.8 m) long
FASTEST SPEED	56 miles per hour (90 km/h)
FOOD CHAIN SNACK	bird
FOOD CHAIN FEAST	musk oxen
KILLER BLOW	is a long-distance hunter that can travel miles to find prey

GRAY WOLF

AVERAGE LENGTH	6.6 feet (2 m)
FASTEST SPEED	37 miles per hour (60 km/h)
FOOD CHAIN SNACK	fish
FOOD CHAIN FEAST	moose
KILLER BLOW	its super-organized pack works as a killing machine

INDIAN WOLF

AVERAGE LENGTH	3 feet (1 m)
FASTEST SPEED	36-38 miles per hour (57-61 km/h)
FOOD CHAIN SNACK	rat
FOOD CHAIN FEAST	antelope
KILLER BLOW	is a super-smart predator that uses its hunting partner as a decoy

ETHIOPIAN WOLF

AVERAGE LENGTH	3 feet (1 m)
FASTEST SPEED	30 miles per hour (48 km/h)
FOOD CHAIN SNACK	rat
FOOD CHAIN FEAST	hare
KILLER BLOW	its body has adapted to survive on only small available prey

HOWL DID WE DO?

GLOSSARY

adapted changed to better suit its environment

ancestor an ancient relative

breed to mate and then produce babies

canid a member of a group of animals that includes wolves, foxes, jackals, and coyotes

climate change the change in temperature and weather over a long period of time

coniferous describes trees that have leaves that do not fall off in winter

continent one of Earth's seven large areas of land including Europe, Asia, Africa, North America, South America, Australia, and Antarctica

critically endangered at great risk of dying out

deciduous describes trees that have leaves that fall off in winter

den a home in which an animal such as a wolf lives and keeps its babies

descended came from an animal that lived in the past

deserts places that receive little or no rainfall

dominant controlling and in charge of others

ecosystems environments and the plants and animals that live in them. All of the things in an ecosystem depend on each other to survive

endangered at risk of dying out

environment the natural world or the natural place in which a plant or animal lives

evolved changed over time to better suit its environment

extinction the process of dying out

fossils the hardened remains of dead animals and plants

genetic related to genes, which determine how a living thing looks and behaves

grasslands areas where a lot of grass grows, but few trees and shrubs

Ice Age one of a number of times in Earth's history when ice and snow covered much of the land

insulated kept warm

mammals animals that give birth to babies and feed them with milk from their bodies

mammoths large elephant-like animals that were covered with hair and that lived during the Ice Age

mate to come together with an animal of the opposite sex but of the same species, to create babies

predator an animal that hunts and eats other animals

prehistoric describes a time before people began to record things, or write them down

prey to hunt and feed on another animal

submits gives in and shows another animal that it is in charge

territory the area that an animal or group of animals considers its own

track to follow prey

FIND OUT MORE

Books

Markle, Sandra. *On the Hunt with Wolves* (Ultimate Predators).
Lerner Publications, 2022.

Martin, Cynthia. *The World of Food Chains with Max Axiom
Super Scientist: 4D An Augmented Reading Science Experience.*
Capstone Publishing, 2019.

Spilsbury, Louise. *Food Chains* (Engage Literacy).
Capstone Publishing, 2021.

Websites

Discover more about wolves at:
https://kids.britannica.com/kids/article/wolf/353930

Discover more about the world's biggest wolf at:
**https://kids.nationalgeographic.com/animals/mammals/facts/
  gray-wolf**

Learn more fascinating facts about wolves at:
https://wolf.org/wolf-info/wild-kids/fun-facts

Publisher's note to educators and parents:
All the websites featured above have been carefully reviewed to
ensure that they are suitable for students. However, many websites
change often, and we cannot guarantee that a site's future contents
will continue to meet our high standards of educational value. Please
be advised that students should be closely monitored whenever they
access the Internet.

INDEX

About the Author

Katherine Eason has written many books about animals and their environments. In researching and writing this book, she has discovered that wolves are incredibly intelligent animals that deserve our respect and protection.